TechBytes
Press
http://www.techbytespress.com

Version 2018.11.30

Disclaimer
Unfortunately in this world of lawsuits, I want to make
the following disclaimer. Everything that I have written about
here is about my own experiences or as a result of research
that I did. Your results may vary from mine. What you will
read about here are steps I have taken for my own
emergency preparations. If I haven't ordered something but

found that it was something that I would be looking at in the future, I will indicate that.

Table of Contents

About The Author

Lisa's job takes her all around the country and occasionally overseas. She has had opportunities to try various cuisines from around the world. With her passion for food, she has found opportunities to go to different cooking schools and get to learn first hand how to cook many of these recipes. She finds it very exciting to learn new recipes and bring them to her home. She would like to share these with you.

Dedication

Thank you Twyla and Will Pace for
sharing your family recipes
that made this book possible.

Breakfast

Chili Rellenos

10 Anaheim peppers, peeled, split on one side
and deseeded
2 to 3 cups cooked seasoned beef
20 whole eggs
Salt and Pepper

To peel Anaheim peppers or any peppers in a hurry,
put them in a fryer basket and dip them into
hot grease, just long enough to blister the skin.
With these peppers for Rellenos, they need to
cook in the hot grease long enough to get semi-soft
Then put them in a sealed baggy for 20 minutes or
so until the skin slips rinse them off under running water
and the skin will come right off

Crack 2 eggs into small bowl
Whisk until well mixed
Salt and pepper to taste
Pour onto flat grill, keeping it about the size
of a round omelet (6 to 7 inches) while it is setting,
place a stuffed pepper in the middle
When the egg is done like an omelet,
fold it over the pepper from both sides
Flip it over until both sides are done
Remove to plate - cover with ranchero sauce

Cheese Grits

2 cups water
1 teaspoon salt
1 cup grits
2 cups milk
1 stick margarine
2 eggs, beaten
1 cup grated cheese
Garlic powder

Cook, grits, water, salt until thick
Add margarine, let melt,
then add milk, eggs, cheese, garlic powder
Bake with pan in water about 326 to 350 oven until set

Jalapeno Cheese Grits

1 gallon and quart milk
2 1/2 cups butter
5 cups grits
1 tablespoons and 2 teaspoon salt
2 1/2 teaspoon white pepper
Another 1 2/3 butter
2/3 cup chopped deseeded Jalapenos
2 1/2 pounds grated cheese

Bring milk to a boil
Add first butter and stirring grits
Cook, stirring consistently, until the mixture
is consistency of oatmeal (about 5 minutes)
Remove grits from heat,
add salt and pepper and beat mixture with mixer

Add remaining butter, jalapenos and stir in cheese
Pour into a greased shallow pan and
cook at 350 degrees for 1 hour
This can be made ahead and
refrigerated until ready to cook

Sam's Cloud Biscuits

2 cup flour
1 tablespoon sugar
4 teaspoon baking powder
1/2 teaspoon salt
1/2 cup shortening
1 beaten egg
2/3 cup milk

Cut shortening into dry ingredients until
mixture resembles coarse crumbs
Combined egg and milk add to flour
mixture all at once
Stir until dough follows Fork around ball
Turn out on lightly floured board and
need 20 Strokes
Roll 3/4 inch thick and cut to desired size
Bake on ungreased sheet at 450 for 10 to 15 minutes

Holiday Breakfast Bake

1 package (12 ounce) bulk pork sausage
1/3 cup chopped onion
1/3 cup chopped green bell pepper
1/3 cup chopped red bell pepper
10 eggs
1 cup shredded cheddar cheese
1 can (16 ounce) Grands Biscuits

Heat oven to 375
Spray 13 by 9 inch glass
baking dish with cooking spray

In 10 inch skillet, brown sausage, onion and
Bell peppers, drain well.

In large bowl, beat eggs
Stir and cheese and sausage mixture
Separate dough into eight biscuits
Press biscuits into bottom of baking dish
Poor sausage mixture over biscuit crust

Bake 25 to 80 minutes or until egg mixture is set and
crust is a deep golden brown
Cool 5 minutes before serving

Biscuit and Gravy Casserole

1 can grand biscuits
1/2 pound ground breakfast sausage
3 tablespoon flour
1/2 teaspoon salt
1/2 teaspoon pepper
2 1/2 cups milk

Preheat oven to 400 degrees
Prepare a small casserole dish with cooking spray
Set aside
Open biscuits and cut biscuits into quarters
Later half of the biscuit quarters in prepared dish
Bake for 10 minutes
Meanwhile, prepare gravy

In a heavy skillet, Brown the ground breakfast sausage
over medium high heat until fully cooked
Sprinkle the cook sausage with three tablespoons flour
Use a wooden spoon to stir flour in a sausage
until completely absorbed

Lower Heat to medium and cook
flour/sausage mixture for 3 to 5 minutes,
stirring frequently

Add milk and stir to combine
Add salt and black pepper

Stir frequently until mixture turns into a slight boil
Taste, adjust seasoning as desired

If the gravy is too thin add some flour.
If the gravy is too thick add some water.

Pour gravy over the cook biscuits
Layered the remaining uncooked quarter biscuits over the gravy

Place dish on baking sheet,
and bake for 20-25 minutes or
until golden brown

Serve immediately

Pancakes

1 1/4 cup flour
2 tablespoon sugar
1 tablespoon baking powder
1/2 teaspoon salt

Mixed together in one bowl

1 slightly beaten egg
1 cup milk
2 tablespoons oil or melted shortening
In small bowl, mix together.

Combine mixture
Cook on hot ungreased griddle
Makes about 10 4" pancakes

German Pancakes

2 cups milk
3/4 cups flour mix all these together
1/2 teaspoon salt
3 eggs
1/ 4 cup melted butter

Melt 1/2 stick butter in 9 inch square pan
Pour batter over butter

Bake at 450 for 25 to 30 minutes
Will rinse and then fall

Slice into pieces and serve with maple syrup
(May also top with slices peaches or
other fruit in season with maple syrup)

Joseph's Waffles

2 cups flour
1/2 teaspoon salt
2 tablespoon sugar
2 eggs separated
1 1/2 cup milk

Mix all dry ingredients in bown, separated yolks and
mix gradually adding milk
Makes into a batter where better is smooth
Then outer fold and stiffly beaten egg whites and
bacon hot waffle iron

Salads

Christmas Pistachio Salad

1 small package pistachio
pudding and pie filling
1 large can crushed pineapple
1 large can fruit cocktail
One small bottle Moschino cherries
2 cups juice from drain fruit
2/3 cups pecans

Drain the pineapple and fruit cocktail,
reserving one cup juice
In large bowl mix together
the fruit and pudding pie filling,
mixing 2 minutes and
add fruit and pecans
Chill before serving

Pork and Bean Salad

1 large can pork and beans
2 chopped hard boiled eggs
1 small chopped onion
2 to 3 medium sized sour pickles, chopped
1/2 teaspoon celery seed

Drain thoroughly one large can
Van Camp's Pork and Beans
Add 2 chopped hard-boiled eggs, onion,
and sour pickles
Add a little salt (very little) and
1/2 teaspoon celery seed.
Mix together with Miracle Whip to moisten well
Chill

This is very good with fish

Will's Blueberry Salad

2 small packages raspberry Jell-O
2 cups boiling water
1 cup blueberries, drained
1 small cam crushed pineapples drained

And chill until firm
Best of made in large shallow dish

Cover with toppings made of
8 oz softened cream cheese
1 carton sour cream
1 cup powdered sugar
1 teaspoon vanilla
Chopped Nuts

Mix well together
Sprinkle chop nuts on top spreading on jelled base
Delicious is a salad or dessert

Mexican Salad

1/2 pound ground beef
1 can ranch style beans
1/2 package taco seasoning mix
1 small head lettuce
1 avocado, chopped
2 tomatoes, chopped
1/3 slices onion, chopped
1/3 jar green olives
Fritos
Cheddar cheese, shredded

Brown and drain ground beef
Add taco seasonings and stir to blend
Add beans and heat
Pour over salad made with lettuce, tomatoes,
onions, avocados and olives
Crush fritos and add along with cheese
Where to blend all ingredients and serve immediately

Orange Salad

2 small packages orange gelatin
2 cups boiling water
1 small can frozen orange juice
1 pint orange sherbet
1 can mandarin oranges

Combine all ingredients, except oranges,
while water is hot
Add orange oranges chill and serve

Potato Salad

8 Irish potatoes
4 boiled eggs
2 slices onion, chopped finely
4 dill pickles, chopped
1/2 cup pickle juice
1/3 jar salad olives
1/2 cup of olive juice
1 cup Miracle Whip
1 teaspoon mustard
Dash garlic salt
Dash freshly ground pepper

Boil potatoes
While still hot, remove skins and coarsely chop
into a large bowl containing pickles,
pickle juice, salad olives, olive juice and onion
Blend well and to all the juice is absorbed
Sprinkle garlic salt and pepper on
top of cooling potatoes
Add eggs, Miracle Whip and mustard
Blend
May need to use more Miracle Whip
Chill well before serving
Sprinkle top of salad with paprika

Hot German Potato Salad

6 medium potatoes
For hard boiled eggs, sliced
6 slices bacon
3/4 cup chopped onion
2 tablespoons flour
2 tablespoons sugar
1/2 teaspoon celery seeds
2 teaspoon pepper
1/2 teaspoon dry mustard
3,/4 cup water
1/3 cup vinegar

Boiled potatoes in jackets until tender, drain
Dry potatoes by shaking in pan over low heat
Peel and cut into 1/4 inch slices
Alternate layers of potatoes and eggs
in two quart casserole dish
Fry bacon slowly, drain and crumble
Saute onion and bacon drippings
until golden brown
Blend dry ingredients into bacon drippings
Cook on low heat, stirring until
smooth and bubbly
Remove from heat, stirring water and vinegar
Return to heat and bring to a boil,
stirring consistently, boil 1 minute
Stirring in bacon
Pour sauce over potatoes
Cover and bake in 350 degree oven for
30 to 35 minutes

Soups, Stews and Chili

Green Chile Stew

1 1/2 cup oil
10 large onions, chopped
2/3 minced garlic
20 pounds boneless pork butt,
cut into 3/4 inch cubes
1 #10 chopped canned tomatoes, undrained
2 quarts chopped green chilies
10 large potatoes,
peeled and cut into 1 inch cubes
5 quarts water
1 1/2 teaspoons Comino
1 1/2 teaspoons dried Mexican Leaf Oregano
1 1/2 teaspoons salt over medium

Heat oil in large pan over medium heat
Add onions and garlic
Cover and cook until onion is soft
but not brown, 4 to 5 minutes
Add pork and cook, uncovered,
stirring occasionally, until meat has lost its pink
Add chopped tomatoes

Add green chilies, potatoes, water, coming and
oregan and bring to boil

Cover, reduce heat and simmer an hour or
until meat is tender
Add salt to taste, starting with 1/2 teaspoon
Uncover and simmer 15 minutes

Beer Bean Soup

1 pound white beans (Navy)
5 cups water
1 meaty ham bone
1 can beer
1 large carrot, chopped
1 medium onion, chopped
1/2 cup chopped parsley
1 tablespoons basil leaves
1/4 salt
1/4 teaspoon pepper
1/4 teaspoon garlic salt

Soak beans overnight, or an hour in boiling water
Cook beans and other ingredients 1 1/2 to 2 hours,
or until done
Also works well in a crock pot

Asparagus Potato Soup

1 (13 3/4 oz) can of chicken broth
4 medium potatoes, pared and chopped
1/3 cup chopped onion
1/2 teaspoon salt
1/8 teaspoon (generous) ground nutmeg
1 can drained asparagus pieces
1 1/2 cup light cream
1 (5 oz) jar Neufchatel cheese spread with
Pimento

In a large saucepan combined chicken broth,
potatoes, onion, salt, and nutmeg
Bring to boil
Reduce heat and simmer, covered,
for 5 to 8 minutes until potatoes are tender
Add asparagus
Blend together light cream and cheese spread
Stir into soup mixture until melted
Do not boil

Cowboy Stew

6 slices bacon; fry and crumble
1 1/2 pound ground beef
1 cup chopped onion
1/2 cup chopped green pepper
Garlic powder to taste

Brown together, then add:

2 can tomatoes
1/2 teaspoon pepper
1 tablespoon chili powder
1 can Ranch Style Beans
1 large can whole kernel corn, drained
1 can potatoes, cubed

Simmer for 45 minutes

Canadian Cheese Soup

1/4 cup butter
1/2 cup chopped onion (fine)
1/2 cup chopped carrots (fine)
1/4 cup (generous) sifted flour
Salt and pepper to taste
1 pint milk
1 pint chicken stock or two cups stock
1 tablespoons cornstarch
1/8 teaspoon baking soda
2 1/2 cups grated cheese

Melt butter in large pot
Saute 1/2 cup chopped onion,
then add the half a cup chopped carrots and
1/4 cup flour,
and mixing lightly
Stir in the chicken stock
Add cornstarch, salt, pepper and baking soda
Mix well
Add cheese and milk which should be at
room temperature
Stir
Serve hot

Broccoli Soup

2 (10 oz) package frozen broccoli,
one chopped and one spears
2 cans condensed cream of mushroom soup
1 1/2 soup cans milk
3/4 soup can dry white wine
4 tablespoons butter or margarine

In large saucepan,
cook broccoli according to package directions
Drain
rough cut spears
Add soup, milk,wine, butter and margarine
Heat through

Country Potato Soup

4 cups diced, Idaho potatoes
1/2 cup diced celery
1/2 cup diced onion
2 cups water
2 chicken bouillon cubes
1/4 teaspoon salt
2 cups milk
1 cups (8 oz) sour cream
1 tablespoon (generous) parsley

In large saucepan combine potatoes, celery, onion,
water, bouillon cube and salt
Cover and cook until vegetables are tender
(20 minutes)

Add 1 cup milk and heat
In medium bowl mix sour cream, flour, parsley,
and remaining cup of milk
Gradually stir some sour cream mixture
into soup base
Cook over low heat, stirring consistently,
until thickened
To hasten thickening break-up tender potatoes
with whisk before adding sour cream mixture

Chili Con Carne

1 1/2 cup cooked pinto beans with juice
1/2 large onion, sliced
1 green pepper, chopped
1 pound ground meat
3 whole cloves
1 medium can V8 juice
1 large can tomatoes
1 tablespoons chili powder
1 teaspoon salt
Generous dash paprika
1 bay leaf

Brown meat and drain
Add everything except beans and simmer
until onion is transparent
Add beans and heat through
Better if can simmer about an hour

Bonanza Beans

1 pound dry pinto beans
1/4 pound diced bacon
1 Clove garlic, diced
3/4 cup onion
3/4 cup green pepper
1/2 cup ketchup
Water
1/2 teaspoon liquid smoke sauce
1/8 teaspoon crushed red pepper
1 teaspoon chili powder
1 teaspoon salt

Wash and sort beans
Soak overnight
Add ingredients and
cook 2 to 3 hours slowly

Chili Blanco

5 pounds small white beans (Navy beans)
3 pounds ground Turkey
1 cup chopped chilis
2 chopped onions
5 cloves garlic, finely chopped
1 tablespoon comino
2 teaspoon salt
1 teaspoon white pepper
1 teaspoon Mexican oregano

Cover 5 lb small white beans
(Navy beans) with chicken broth
Cook 2 to 3 hours until tender
Add more broth is necessary
Then add turkey, green chilis, onions, garlic,
comino, salt, white pepper, Mexican oregano
Simmer 30 to 45 minutes longer and
adjust seasonings as necessary
Be sure to stir the Turkey well after adding
the beans so it doesn't clump together

Family Favorites

Weiners and Potatoes

Weiners
Mashed potatoes
Onions
Cheese

Split wieners lengthwise
Fill with mashed potatoes, chopped onions and
top with cheese
Bake it at about 350 degrees or
until hot and cheese starts to melt

This a favorite of kids

Will and Seth's pizza

Dough:
1 package yeast
1 1/4 cup warm water
3 1/2 to 4 cups flour
1/2 teaspoon salt
1 tablespoon oil

Place Yeast in warm water
Let rest 5 minutes
Allow to dissolve
Add oil and salt and stir
Add flour needs the last 1/2 teaspoon to 3/4 cups
Cover bowl for 30 minutes

Divided in half and
turn out into two pizza pans for thick crust

Divided among three pizza pans for thin crust

Toppings:
1 Cup tomato sauce / pizza sauce
Oregano
Parsley flakes
1 package dry Italian spaghetti sauce mix
Parmesan cheese
Onion, chopped
green peppers, chopped
Ripe olives, sliced
Mozarella cheese, grated

Spread tomato sauce on each crust
Equal amounts of oregano, bacon bits, and parsley
Sprinkle generous amounts of onion, green pepper,

olives and mushrooms
Add cooked drained meat.
Top with mozzarella

Let bake for 20 minutes at 500 degrees
Freezes well

Chicken Spaghetti

4 chicken breasts cut into bite size pieces
1 package spaghetti
1 small can tomato sauce
1 small can pimentos, chopped
3/4 pound grated cheese
1 cup milk
2 cubes chicken bouillon
2 cans cream of mushroom soup
1/2 pound sliced mushroom
1/2 onion, chopped
15 sliced ripe olives
1 green pepper, chopped
4 tablespoons bacon grease
Garlic, salt and pepper to taste

Cook spaghetti in broth,
adding water if necessary
Do not drain
Add remaining ingredients to large pot
containing chicken, water and spaghetti
Mix well placed in greased casserole and
bake at 300 for 1 hour
Stir several times with in baking
Cool 30 minutes before serving
Can be cooked on top of the stove is turned off
in about 30 minutes

Mexican Casserole

3 cans Rotel tomatoes and green chilies
2 cans cream of mushroom soup
2 cans ranch Style beans
1/2 can (small) jalapeno peppers
1/4 pound chunked cheese
1 pound ground hamburger meat
Tortillas

Mix all the above with browned
hamburger meat. (Seasoned)
In a large baking dish layer large pan
with meat mixture, cheese and tortillas

Bake at 325 until hot and bubbly

Ratcliff's King Ranch Casserole

4 boneless chicken breast
Tortilla chips

Mix together:
1 can cream of mushroom soup
1 can cheddar cheese soup
1 medium onion chopped
1 can Rotel tomatoes and chilies
1 cup chicken broth
(mix together and heat in microwave)
Grated cheese

Cook chicken breast.
Place a layer of tortilla chips the bottom
of the pan or casserole dish
Add a layer or chicken
Pour the soup mixture over chicken and tortilla chips
Put grated cheese on top
Cook covered about 30 to 35 minutes in
350 degree oven
Then cook uncovered for an
additional 10 minutes

Serve with additional tortilla chips

Hominy Casserole

2 cans hominy (1 white, 1 yellow)
(Drain one but not the other)
1 small carton sour cream
1 can green chilies
Salt and pepper to taste

Pour all ingredients in a 3 quart casserole dish

Cover with lots of grated cheese
Bake 1 hour at 350

Broccoli & Rice Casserole

1 stick margarine
1/2 cup chopped onion
2 packages chopped broccoli
1 jar (small) cheese whiz
7 oz. Package minute rice
1 can cup cream of chicken soup

Saute onion in margarine
Add broccoli and cheese whiz
Cook Minute Rice as directed on package
Add soup
Mix all ingredients in 2 quart Casserole dish
Bake at 350 until bubbly

Cabbage Casserole

1 medium head cabbage
1/2 cup milk
1 can cream of mushroom soup
2 cups diced ham
1/2 cup bread crumbs

Steam cabbage
arrange ham and cabbage in layers
using two quart casserole
Blend soup and milk,
pour over cabbage and ham mixture.
Top with Crumbs

Bake in 350 degree oven for 3 minutes

Cabbage Rotel

1 pound hamburger
1 head cabbage
2 cans Rotel
1 large onion
1 small can of tomato sauce

Saute hamburger and onion together
When lightly cooked, place chopped cabbage
on top of hamburger
Cook about 10 minutes
Pour Rotel and tomato sauce on top of cabbage
Cook as you like to the doneness of the cabbage

Mexican Fiesta Stackup

4 pounds ground beef
1 1/2 onions, chopped
3 cans Rotel tomatoes and green chili's
4 tablespoons chili powder
2 teaspoons cumin
2 (15 oz) cans tomato sauce
1 teaspoon garlic powder
6 teaspoons salt
2 (25 oz) cans Ranch Style Beans
    (or home cooked pinto beans)

Ground beef, onions and rain
Add everything except the beans
Simmer 1 and 1/2 hours
Before serving, add beans and serve.

Serve in this order:
60 oz. Crushed Fritos
1 (28 oz) box minute rice
(or cook 5 cups regular rice)

Sauce for the meat:
2 tablespoons grated cheese
2 chopped onions
1 large head shredded lettuce
8 tomatoes, chopped
2 or 3 cans chopped ripe olives
1 (14 oz) package coconut
1 (16 oz) jar picante sauce
2 cups chopped pecans

Tagilong Meat Dish

2 pounds lean ground beef
1 onion, chopped
1 tablespoon chili pepper
1 small package wide noodles
1 cup ripe onions (chopped)
1 green pepper (chopped)
1 large can tomatoes
1 #2 can cream style corn
Grated cheese

Sauteed onions, pepper and meat
Drain excess grease off
Cook noodles according to package directions
Drain
Mix all ingredients together, seasoning as desired
You may substitute garlic salt for plain salt
Place in casserole with grated cheese on top
bake at 350 for 40 to 50 minutes

Chicken Divan

6 chicken breast
boiled deboned and turn into bite-size pieces
3 package frozen chopped broccoli
Cooked as directed and drained well
1/2 pound fresh mushrooms
sliced and sauteed in margarine

In 9 x 13 baking dish spread first broccoli,
then chicken, then mushrooms

In bowl, mix together
2/3 cup mayonnaise
2 teaspoon lemon juice
1 1/4 teaspoon curry powder
2 cans cream of mushroom soup
1/2 cup milk

Pour over chicken
Then sprinkle with grated cheese over the top.

Bake at 350 for 35 minutes

Chicken Paprika

1 chicken, stewed, boned and rough chopped
1/4 cup butter
1/2 green pepper, chopped
1 can tomatoes, broken up
2 stalks celery
2 slices onion, chopped
Fresh mushrooms, sliced and sauteed
1 can cream of mushroom soup
1 tablespoons paprika
1/8 tablespoon red pepper
1 teaspoon garlic salt
1 teaspoon Worcestershire sauce
1 package Noodles

In large Skillet, saute onion, celery,
peppers and mushrooms in butter
Add chicken and tomatoes
Simmer 10 minutes covered
Add remaining ingredients in heat just
to boiling point
Serve hot over buttered noodles

Sausage Lasagna

3/4 of a 10 ounce package lasagna noodles
1 pound mozzarella cheese, sliced
1 pound sausage, browned and drained
1 clove garlic, minced
1 tablespoon basil
1 tablespoon garlic salt
1 pound fresh tomatoes, chopped
12 oz can tomato paste
2 eggs
2 cups cottage cheese or ricotta cheese
1/2 cup parmesan cheese
Salt and pepper to taste

Cook, drain and cool noodles
Simmer together for 30 minutes cooked sausage,
garlic cloves, salt, basil, tomatoes and
tomato paste
Add eggs, cottage cheese, parsley,
salt and pepper, mixing well
Layer in large dish,
beginning with small amount of sauce
Place Mozarella between all layers
Bake at 375 for 30 minutes

Salmon Croquettes

1 can (15 Oz) can salmon
1 medium onion, finely chopped
1 tablespoon parsley flakes
1 egg
3 tablespoons chopped green pepper
6 saltine crackers

Remove bone and dark skin from salmon, flake
Add minced onions parsley flakes, egg
and crackers
Mix well by hand
if too thin add in two or three more crackers
Should feel solid enough to form into
golf size balls but try not dry
Roll in crushed saltine crackers crumbs
Deep fry in hot crisco oil

Chow Mein Tuna

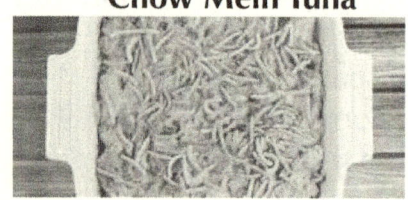

1 small can tuna, flaked
1 can cream of celery soup
1/2 soup can milk
2 tablespoons onions
1 can green peas
1 can chow mein noodles
2 hard boiled eggs, chopped

And large saucepan combine tuna,
soup, milk, onion, eggs and peas
Heat through, serve hot over Chow Mein noodles
or try rice noodles

Chalupa Roast

After Ingredients Added

Roast when finished

One four pound boneless rump roast
Coat all sides with chili powder

Put in the bottom of a slow cooker
and layer the following:

1 chopped onion
2 cups dry pinto beans
2 cans rotel tomatoes
1 can cream.of mushroom soup

1 can chopped green chilis
1 1/2 teaspoon oregano
2 teaspoon salt
1 1/2 cup water

Cook for 12 to 16 hours
DO NOT STIR UNTIL TIME IS UP

After cooking, stirring all together and
roast should shred
Eat with flour tortillas like a burrito or
just eat with homemade bread and a salad

Tuna on a Shoestring

2 cups shredded carrots
2 cups chopped celery
1/2 cup chopped onion
1 can tuna (or try chicken)
1/2 cup miracle whip
1 small can Shoestring potatoes

Combined All Above, except for Shoestring potatoes
Chill
Add Shoestring potatoes just before serving

Texas Five Alarm Chili

2 pounds ground beef
8 ounces tomato sauce
16 ounce water
6 tablespoons ground chili pepper
1 1/2 teaspoon ground cumin
1 1/2 teaspoon ground oregano
1 1/2 teaspoon salt
1 1/2 teaspoon minced onion
1 1/2 teaspoon minced garlic
1 1/2 teaspoon paprika
3/4 teaspoon cayenne pepper
1 1/2 teaspoon cornstarch

Brown meat in large saucepan
Add tomato sauce and water
Mix well
Stir in all spices and simmer
In a small bowl, mix cornstarch with
some warm water to make a paste
Add paste to chili and stir
Allow chili to simmer for 45 minutes
Stir occasionally

Cola Steaks

1 cup cola
1/2 cup soy sauce
2 tablespoons Dijon Mustard
1 tablespoon horseradish
2 cloves garlic, minced
1 teaspoon ground black pepper
2 pounds sirloin steak

Whisk together Cola, soy sauce,
Dijon mustard, horseradish, garlic and
black pepper in a bowl and
pour into resealable plastic bag

Add steak, coat with the marinade
Squeeze out excess air and seal in bag
Marinate in refrigerator for 24 hours

Preheat heat to 400 degrees
Remove steak from resealable bag and
discard remaining marinade

Cook steak on a preheated Grill to
desired doneness about 5 minutes per side

Seafood

Deviled Crab

6 large eggs
1 1/2 cups chopped green onion
1/3 cup fresh lemon juice
1/4 teaspoon ground nutmeg
2 tablespoons grated lemon rind
1 pound fresh lump crabmeat, drained
1 1/2 cups butter, melted and divided
5 cups soft breadcrumbs, divided
1 cup chopped fresh parsley
1/2 teaspoon salt
1/4 teaspoon freshly ground pepper

Combine first 6 ingredients in a large bowl
Add 1 cup melted butter, 4 cups breadcrumbs and
next 3 ingredients
Spoon crabmeat mixture into 10 baking shells

Top serving evenly with remaining breadcrumbs,
drizzle with remaining 1/2 cup melted butter
Bake, uncovered 400 degrees for 20 minutes or
until thoroughly heated
Turn oven setting to broil
Broil 3 minutes or until golden brown
Serve immediately

Broiled Shrimp

2 pounds shrimp
1/2 cup margarine
2 tablespoons lemon juice
2 tablespoons Worcestershire Sauce
1 tablespoons Jamaican Choice Tropical
Or Pineapple Sauce
1/4 teaspoon red pepper
1/2 teaspoon salt
Hot French Bread

Wash, peel and devein shrimp
Melt margarine in saucepan
Add lemon juice, Worcestershire sauce,
pepper sauce, red pepper and salt
Let it simmer 5 to 10 minutes
Place raw shrimp in a 9x12x2 baking pan
Place on next to lowest rack in oven
Broil 20 minutes, turning shrimp every 5 minutes
Serve in gravy with plenty of hot
French Bread for "dunking"

Fiesta Shrimp

5 medium cucumbers, peeled seeded
and coarsely chopped
2 1/2 red bell peppers, diced
2 1/2 green bell peppers, diced
2 1/2 small purple onion, finely chopped
20 diced Roma tomatoes
2 quarts tomato juice
2 tablespoons chopped
1/2 cup minced jalapenos (deseeded)
3 tablespoons lime juice
2 1/2 teaspoons pepper
1 1/2 teaspoons pepper
1 1/2 pounds small cooked shrimp
1 cup olive oil
2 tablespoons sugar
Cilantro for garnish

Mixed together in a large non aluminum ball,
refrigerate at least 4 hours before serving
Serve cold and chill bowls with cilantro for garnish

Shrimp Scampi

1 stick margarine
1 to 2 pounds peeled shrimp
1 teaspoon paprika
Garlic cloves to taste
1/2 to 1 red pepper
1 onion sliced thin
1 bell pepper, sliced thin

Melt butter in large skillet
Saute onion and bell peppers in butter
Add garlic, shrimp, paprika and pepper
Simmer over medium heat for 4 to 5 minutes
until shrimp is done

Shrimp Au Gratin

2 stick margarine
1/2 to 1 cup chopped onions
1 stalk celery, chopped
1/2 teaspoon red pepper
1 chopped bell pepper
1 pound shrimp (peeled and cleaned)
1/2 cup flour
1/2 pound grated cheddar cheese
2 egg yolks
Salt
1 13 ounce can evaporated milk

Melt margarine and onions, celery, bell pepper
Add flour and milk
Beat egg yolks and add milk
Then add to flour mixture and cook 5 minutes,
stirring frequently
Add seasonings and shrimp
Grate cheese and add 3/4 of it to sauce
Pour mixture into 13×9 pan and top with leftover cheese
Cover with foil and bake at 350 for 30 to
45 minutes (until firm)

Shrimp and Grits

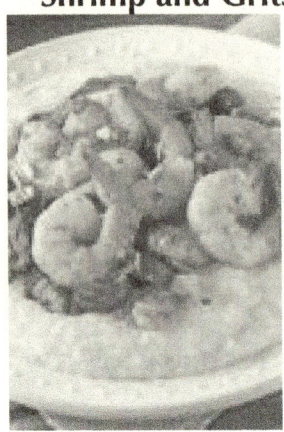

3 cups chicken broth
1 cup uncooked quick cooking grits
1/2 teaspoon salt
1/4 teaspoon freshly ground pepper
2 tablespoons butter
2 cups (8 ounce) shredded cheese
6 slices bacon
1 tablespoon lemon juice
2 pounds medium shrimp, peeled and deveined
2 teaspoons Worcestershire sauce
2 tablespoons fresh parsley
6 green onions
2 garlic cloves

Bring chicken broth to boil over medium-high heat;
stir in grits
Cook, stirring occasionally, 5 to 7 minutes or
until thickened
Remove from heat; stir in salt, pepper,
butter, and cheese.
Set aside and keep warm

Cook bacon in a large non stick skillet over
medium high heat 3 minutes or until crisp;

remove bacon from pan

Cook shrimp in same pan over medium
high heat for about 3 minutes or until almost pink,
stirring occasionally
Add lemon juice, Worcestershire sauce, parsley,
onions and garlic
Cook minutes 3 minutes
Stir in bacon

Spoon grits onto individual plates or
into shallow bowls, top with Shrimp mixture
Serve immediately

Coconut Shrimp with
Orange Chili Dipping Sauce

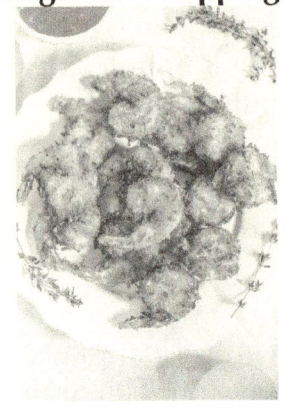

Shrimp
1 pound large shrimp, peeled and
deveined with tail on
1/2 cup flour
Salt and pepper to taste
2 large eggs, beaten
1 cup sweetened shredded coconut
3/4 cup Panko breadcrumbs
About 2 cups canola,
vegetable or coconut oil for frying

Sauce
1/2 cup orange marmalade
1/3 cup sweet Thai chili sauce
salt to taste
Cayenne pepper to taste

Clean the shrimp and set aside
In a small bowl, add the flour, salt and
pepper, stir to combine, set aside
In a separate small bowl,
add the eggs and beat, set aside

In a separate medium Bowl, add the coconut,
and panko
Combine and set aside

In a dutch oven or large skillet,
add the oil and heat over medium heat
While oil heats up begin the battering process

Dip 1 shrimp in flour, dip in egg, and
then dip into coconut-panko mixture,
 pressing it as needed to ensure shrimp
is well coated.

After all shrimp has been battered begin frying
For best result fry in oil 325 to 350 degrees
Wait till oil is hot begin frying

Add the shrimp and small batches to the hot oil,
frying for about 2 to 4 minutes,
until golden brown.

After frying, remove from oil, lay on some paper towels,
and continue the frying process until
all shrimp have been fried

Sauce

In a small bowl, add marmalade,
Thai chili sauce, salt, cayenne pepper,
stir to combine, taste and adjust ratios as desired
Serve shrimp and sauce immediately

Garlic Crab Legs

3 1/2 pounds Alaskan King crab legs with shell
6 years fresh corn
1 1/2 cups butter
3 teaspoon minced garlic
1/9 teaspoon crushed red pepper flakes
1 teaspoon Old Bay Seasoning

In a large pot bring a large amount of
water to boil
Place crab legs and corn in the
pot of boiling water
Boil until the corn is tender and
the crab legs are opaque and flakey
The crab may finish cooking before the corn
Check corn and crab every 5 minutes to
see if they are finished cooking.

When finished cooking, drain well
Cut a slit into each of the crab legs to
make it easier for your guests to get to the meat

In a large saucepan, melt butter, garlic,
red better, and Old Bay Seasoning
Stir in the crab and corn, and
saute them for 5 to 10 minutes

Serve very hot

Breads

Wonderful Sour Dough Biscuits

5 cups flour
5 teaspoons baking powder
1 teaspoon baking soda
1/3 cup sugar
1 package dry yeast
2/3 cups cooking oil
2 1/2 cups buttermilk

Mix dry ingredients
Mix buttermilk and oil
It's often used in warm water
Mix use with buttermilk and oil
Add liquid ingredients to dry ingredients
Mix well
Pour dough out on generously floured board
Knead until no longer sticky
Cut out biscuits bake for 15 minutes in
a 400-degree oven

Jalapeno Cornbread

1 cups sifted flour
1/4 cup sugar
4 teaspoons baking powder
1 cup yellow cornmeal
1/4 teaspoons garlic powder
2 eggs
1 cup milk
1/4 cup soft shortening
1 cup finely chopped onion
1 can (8 oz.) Cream style corn
2 tablespoons chopped cooked jalapenos

Sift together flour, sugar, baking powder,
salt and garlic powder and stir into cornmeal
Add eggs milk and shortening
Beat until smooth
Add onion corn and pepper
Mix well
Pour into greased 9 x 9 x 2 pan
Bacon 425 oven for 35 to 40 minutes

Hot Rolls

3 tablespoons sugar
1 tablespoon salt
1 package yeast
3 tablespoons melted shortening
2 cups lukewarm water
6 cups flour

Dissolve yeast, sugar and salt in water and
melted shortening
Stir in 3 cups flour
Put rest of flour on pastry cloth and
need into dough
Grease large bowls and turned out into it
so it stopped will be coated
Let It Rise until double in bulk
Punch down refrigerator until ready to
make out rules
Let it rise in pan and bake at
350 until light brown

Cornbread

3/4 cups cornmeal
1/4 cup flour
2 tablespoons baking powder
1/4 teaspoon salt
1 tablespoon sugar
1 egg
3/4 cup milk
1/4 cup melted shortening

Melt shortening in iron skillet coating
sides of skillet
Sift dry ingredients into beaten egg and milk
Add shortening
Pour into hot skillet and bake in 450 degree
oven for 20 to 25 minutes

Twyla's Homemade Bread

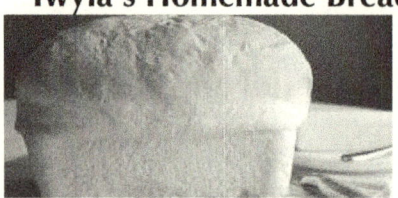

1 package dry yeast
3 cups flour
1 1/4 cups warm water
2 tablespoons oil
2 tablespoons sugar
1 teaspoon salt

Sprinkle yeast in warm water in a large bowl.
Let's set five minutes
Stir to dissolve
Add oil, sugar and salt
Add half of flour, working it with hand mixer
Work rest of flour in by hand
Cover and let it rise for 30 minutes
Punch down 25 times and turn
into a greased loaf pan
Cover and let rise until double
Let rest for 20 minutes
Bake at 375 approximately 30 minutes or
until browned
Well sound hollow when wrapped with Knuckles
Turn out too cool on rack
Brush tablespoon of butter for soft crust
For hard crust brush with milk

Breakfast Bread

1 pound mild or hot sausage, cooked and drained
8 eggs, beaten
2 cups grated cheddar cheese
1/2 green pepper chopped
1 small can green chilies
1 large Grands Biscuits cut into small cubes

Mix all ingredients
Put in well greased Bundt or long loaf pan

Cook at 350 degrees for 35 to 40 minutes

Cinnamon Spiral Bread

1/2 cup water
1 package dry yeast
2 cups lukewarm water
2 cups quick cooking oats
2 tablespoons soft shortening
1 tablespoon salt
1 cup raisins
5 1/2 to 6 cups sifted flour

Dissolve yeast in water in mixing bowl
Stir in milk, rolled oats, brown sugar,
shortening, salt, raisins and half the flour
Mixed with spoon until smooth
Add rest of flour, mix by hand
Turn onto lightly lightly floured board
Knead until smooth and elastic, about 5 minutes.

Ground up into grease pool,
bring grease Side Up
Let rise on warm plate until doubled in bulk,
about one-and-a-half to two hours
Divide dough into two parts
Roll up into a ball
Each into an oblong 15 by 8 sprinkle with all
except two tablespoons of mixture and half a
cup sugar and 2 teaspoon cinnamon
Roll up like a jelly-roll ceiling tightly
Place in to greased loaf pans
Let it rise until about double in bulk
Allow about 40 to 50 minutes

Heat oven to 400 and bake 35 to 40 minutes

Brush type of hot bread with corn syrup and
sprinkle with the rest of cinnamon sugar mixture

Desserts

Cliffy Red Velvet Cake

3 oz unsweetened chocolate (Chopped)
2 cups granulated sugar
4 large eggs
1 1/4 cups vegetable oil
1 1/2 teaspoon pure vanilla
2 cups all-purpose flour
2 1/4 teaspoons baking soda
1/4 teaspoon salt
36 Oz Can beets (drained and pureed)
1 teaspoon red food coloring
2 cups heavy cream
12 oz cream cheese (room temperature)
12 oz mascarpone cheese
1/2 teaspoon vanilla extract
One and a half cups powdered sugar

Preheat oven to 350 degrees
Melting chocolate in a metal bowl and
set over saucepan of boiling water or
on the top of a double boiler
(or melt in microwave 20 to 30 seconds)

Meanwhile, place the sugar, eggs, oil and
vanilla and mix for about 1 minute on a low speed
In a mixing bowl, sift together the flour,
baking soda and salt
Add the dry ingredients to egg mixture and
continue to mix on low speed
until well incorporated.

Add melted chocolate and mix on low speed,
then add the beets and food coloring
Continue to mix on low speed until

all the ingredients are combined
Divide the batter evenly between 3 greased
flour pans and bake for 20 to 25 minutes or
until cake springs back when touched or
when a toothpick comes out clean

Cool for 10 minutes in the pans,
then turn the layers out on a rack
to cool completely

Icing

For the heavy cream into a small bowl and
whip into soft peaks
Refrigerate
Place the cream cheese in a bowl
on low speed until soft and smooth

Add mascarpone and mix until well combined
Add half the vanilla and powdered sugar
and mix well
Fold into the whipped cream by hand with
a spatula
add the rest of the powdered sugar and vanilla
refrigerate until ready to assemble

Sad Cake

1 (1 pound box brown sugar)
2 cups bisquick
4 eggs
1 cups chopped pecans

Mix well and spread in oblong baking pan
Bake at 350 for 30 minutes
The cake will rise during baking but
fall as it cools
Thus, the name "Sad Cake"

Banana Pudding

1/2 cup sugar
1 egg
2 tablespoons flour
1 1/2 cup milk
2 tablespoons butter
1 tablespoon vanilla
Bananas
Vanilla wafers

Add flour to Sugar
Add egg and stir well
Add half milk and blend
Then add remaining milk and cook
Stirring constantly until thickened

Makes enough pudding sauce for two
slice bananas in about 2 cups of wafers fills an 8 x 8 dish

Seth's Sugar Cookies

1 cup shortening
1 cup sugar
2 eggs, beaten
2 1/2 cups flour
1 teaspoon baking powder
1/4 teaspoon salt
2 teaspoons vanilla

Cream shortening and sugar
Add beaten eggs, flour sifted with
baking powder and salt
Add vanilla
Chill
Dough may be rolled 1/4 inch thick and cut,
or using cookie press
Cookies can also be drop by teaspoons on
greased cookie sheet

Bake at 350 for about 10 minutes
Makes about 6 dozen cookies

Will's Chocolate Oatmeal Cookies

4 tablespoons cocoa
2 cups sugar
1 stick margarine
1/2 cup sugar
1/2 cup milk
1/2 cup peanut butter
1 teaspoon vanilla
3 cups uncooked 1 minute oatmeal

Bring cocoa, sugar, margarine and
oil to boil in a large saucepan
Boil 1 minute
Remove from heat and add
peanut butter, vanilla and oatmeal
Stir well to mix
Drop by Spoonful on wax paper
Cool

Granddad Lynn's Deer Hunting Cobbler

1 stick margarine
2 large cans sliced peaches
1 small can crushed pineapple
1 box yellow cake mix
Dash or two of nutmeg

Melt margarine in 9 ×13 pan.
Mix together the peaches, pineapples,
nutmeg, a little sugar, if needed and
about 2 tablespoons cake mix
Pour on top of margarine in pan
Bake in 350 oven for 30 to 40 minutes
Prick holes in cobbler when halfway done
so juice can bubble through
About 10 minutes before it is done
Sprinkle a little sugar on top and
cook until lightly browned

Pie cherries can also be used for this
Add 3/4 cup sugar to 1 can cherries and
1 tablespoon almond extract
You will need 3 cans of cherries

Snickerdoodles

1 cup soft softened shortening
  (Equal parts mixed crisco and margarine)
1 1/2 cups sugar
2 eggs
2 teaspoon cream of tarter
1 teaspoon baking soda
1/4 teaspoon salt
2 tablespoons sugar
2 teaspoons cinnamon

Heat oven to 400
Make shortening sugar and eggs thoroughly
Sift together the flour, cream of tartar,
baking soda, salt and stir in
Form dough into balls into the size of a walnut
Each ball a mixture of two tbsp sugar
and cinnamon
Place about 2 inches apart on ungreased
cookie sheet
Bake 8 to 10 minutes
Makes about 5 dozen cookies

Twyla's Brownies

1/2 cup softened margarine
6 tablespoons cocoa
3/4 cup flour
1/2 teaspoon baking powder
1/4 teaspoon salt
2 eggs
2 teaspoons Karo
1 cup sugar
1 tablespoon vanilla
1 cup chopped nuts

Beat egg whites with sugar until fluffy
Add Karo and mix
Sift flour with baking powder, salt and Coco
Add vanilla and nuts
Bacon grease and floured pan in
350 oven for 30 minutes

Apple Chimichangas

One can apple pie filling
Tortillas

Spin about 1/3 cup Apple mixture
down center of tortilla
Fold the sides like making a burrito
Secure with a wooden pick and
place folded side on a lightly greased baking sheet
Baked chimichangas at 450 degrees for
10 minutes or until golden brown
Serve hot with choice of toppings

Toppings:
Vanilla ice cream, caramel sauce, toasted pecans

7 Up Cake

2 sticks margarine
1/2 cup Crisco
2 3/4 cups sugar
5 eggs, beaten well
One small bottle of 7-Up (7 oz)
2 teaspoons vanilla

Cream shortening well
add sugar a little at a time
Add sifted flour and 7-Up a little at a time
(hold close to batter)
Add well beaten eggs, vanilla and pinch of salt
Pour into a well greased and
floured stem cake pan.

Bake at 350 for 45 minutes,
reduce heat to 300 for 5 minutes more
Let stand in pan 10 minutes
before removing from pan

Seth's Thirty Cupcakes

1 chocolate cake mix
1 tablespoon Karo for moistness

Follow chocolate cake mix directions
Pour into muffin liners, filling only half full
Mixed together the following and
spent about 3/4 teaspoon in the
center of each batter filled liner

1 8 oz cream cheese
1/2 cup powdered sugar
1 egg
1 6 oz package chocolate chips

Bake muffins is directed
Cake will bake up around filling
Cupcakes do not have to be iced
Freezes well

Honey Devil's Food Cake

1/2 cup butter
3/4 cup honey
1/2 cup sugar
3 eggs (separated)
1/2 teaspoons baking soda
1/2 teaspoon salt
1 teaspoon vanilla
1/2 cup walnuts
1 3/4 cup coffee
1 3/4 cup Flour
1/2 teaspoon cinnamon
1/2 cup cocoa

Cream butter, add honey, sugar and egg yolks
Beat until mixture is consistent
Stir in nuts and vanilla
Sift dry ingredients together and beat egg whites
To the creamed mixture,
add dry ingredients alternatively with coffee,
stirring into a batter is smooth
Fold in egg whites and pour into greased pans

Bake at 350 for 35 to 40 minutes or until done

Hershey Bar Cake

8 small plain Hershey bars
2 sticks margarine
2 cup sugar
Four eggs
2 1/2 cup flour
1 cup buttermilk
1/4 baking soda
2 teaspoons vanilla

Cream margarine and sugar
Add eggs, one at a time
Melt Hershey bars with 2 tablespoons hot water,
then add to mixture
Mix baking soda and flour then add
alternately with buttermilk to the first mixture
Stir in vanilla bake at 350 oven for 1 hour or
until well done

Grandmother Myra's Jam Cake

1 cup shortening
1 cup sugar
3 cups flour
1 teaspoon salt
2 teaspoons baking powder
One cup seedless blackberry jam

Mixing usual manner. Mix and have ready:
     1 cup raisins
     1 cup pecans
     1 cup coconut

Add this mixture to cake mixture
Baking sheet cake pan at 350 in oven
for 35 to 40 minutes

Grandma Brook's Gingerbread

1/2 cup sugar
1 cup black molasses
(Brer Rabbit - do not substitute)
1/2 cup margarine
1 teaspoons cinnamon
1 teaspoon Ginger
1/4 teaspoon cloves
2 teaspoons soda
(Dissolved in 1 cup boiling water)
2 cups flour
2 well beaten eggs

Mix ingredients in order listed
Dough is very soft
Bake in a 13 x 9 x 2 baking dish in 350 oven
for 35 to 40 minutes
Very good served with whipped cream or
Cool Whip or with butter while cake is still hot

Spider Cake

1/3 cup butter or margarine
1/2 cup brown sugar (packed)
Pineapple slices
Maraschino Cherries
Pecan Halves
2 eggs
2/3 cup sugar
6 tablespoons juice from pineapple
1 teaspoon vanilla
1 cup sifted flour
1/3 teaspoon baking soda
1/4 teaspoon salt

Heat oven to 350
Melt butter and heavy 10-inch Skillet, or baking dish
Sprinkle brown sugar over evenly
Arrange pineapple slices over butter sugar mixture
Garnish with Maraschino cherries in center of
pineapple slices in a Range pecan has
around the pineapple slices beat eggs,
until thick and lemon colored gradually beat in
the sugar beet and juice from fruit and vanilla
Stir together remaining ingredients and
beat these into the mixture
Pour batter over fruit
Bake 45 minutes or until toothpick stuck in
Center of the cake comes out clean
Immediately turn upside down on serving plate
Leave pan over cake for a few minutes
Served warm with plain or whipped cream, if desired

The 1920s marked the beginning of the real cake era
This pineapple upside down cake was known as

a "spider" or "Skillet cake" because it we used to be
and sometimes still is baked in an iron skillet

Almond Joy Cake

1 (18.5 oz) package devils food cake
1 (12 oz) can evaporated milk
2 1/2 cups white sugar
25 large marshmallows
14 oz. flaked coconut
1/2 cup butter
2 cups semisweet chocolate chips
3 oz. Toasted almonds

Mix cake mix and bake as directed for
one 9x13 inch cake

In saucepan combined half a can of milk and
1 1/2 cup sugar
Bring mixture to Rapid boil
Quickly remove from heat and add marshmallows
Stir well until melted
Stir in coconut

Pour mixture on top of cake

In saucepan combine remaining sugar and
the remaining milk
Bring to boil
Remove from heat and add butter and

chocolate chips
Stir until melted
Stirring almonds
Pour mixture on top of coconut topped cake
Chill for at least 2 hours before serving
Cake tastes best of baked the day before

Texas Pictures

Some of lisa's fondest memories are going Shrimping with Uncle ralph outside of Galveston, Texas. His wife, Fay, would lovingly cook the catch of the day in restaurant/bar known as Ralph's place.

Lisa first teaching job

Your Journey starts now

I have left some pages available for you to put your favorite recipes from your travels. Start adding your own to this collection.

Recipe _____

Recipe _____

Recipe _____

Recipe

Recipe _____

Recipe _____

Recipe _____

Recipe _____

Recipe _____

Recipe _____

_____

_____

_____

_____

_____

_____

_____

_____

_____

_____

_____

_____

_____

_____

Recipe _____

Recipe

Recipe _____

Recipe

Recipe _____

_____

_____

_____

_____

_____

_____

_____

_____

_____

_____

_____

_____

_____

_____

_____

Recipe _____

_____

_____

_____

_____

_____

_____

_____

_____

_____

_____

_____

_____

_____

_____

_____

Recipe _____

Recipe

Recipe _____

Recipe _____

Recipe _____

_____

_____

_____

_____

_____

_____

_____

_____

_____

_____

_____

_____

_____

_____

_____

_____

Recipe _____

Recipe

Recipe _____

_____

_____

_____

_____

_____

_____

_____

_____

_____

_____

_____

_____

_____

_____

_____

Recipe _____

Recipe _____

Recipe _____

_____

_____

_____

_____

_____

_____

_____

_____

_____

_____

_____

_____

_____

_____

_____

Recipe _____

Recipe _____

Recipe _____

_____

_____

_____

_____

_____

_____

_____

_____

_____

_____

_____

_____

_____

_____

_____

Made in the USA
Coppell, TX
28 June 2021

58253000R00083